THE CANTERVILLE GHOST

OSCAR

2005, licensed for:
Bildungshaus Schulbuchverlage
Westermann Schroedel Diesterweg
Schönigh Winklers GmbH
Georg-Westermann-Allee 66
38104 Braunschweig
Germany

This edition published by Richmond Publishing® 2006

ISBN:84-668-0836-1
ISBN:3-425-71902-5

Printed in Italy by Techno Media Reference

Adaptation, text and exercises: Barbara Chatwin

Editing: Maureen McLaughlan

Illustrations: Ginetta Ioni

Richmond PUBLISHING

Diesterweg®

The Canterville Ghost

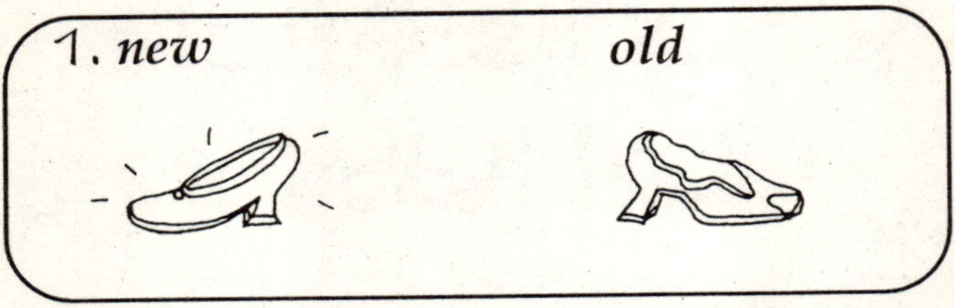

"This is your new[1] home," Mr Otis says to his children. "Ohhhhh!" the twins[2] repeat. "It's very big! Is there a ghost?" "Oh yes," their father replies. "The ghost is very famous[3]!"

ACTIVITY

✎ **Join the opposites.**

NEW	FATHER
BIG	NO
MOTHER	OLD
YES	SMALL

✎ **Fill in the gaps with the words.**

"Hello. My name's David. I'm 10 years .... My ....'s name is Tom and my ....'s name is Ann. Our house isn't small, it's very .... It isn't a .... house, it's very old but I like it very much."

Simon de Canterville, the ghost, sees the Otis family arrive. "Oh no," he thinks. "CHILDREN in my house! I don't like children. They are silly[1] and noisy[2]... and afraid[3] of ghosts!"

1. *silly*

2. *noisy*

3. *afraid*

ACTIVITY

✎ **Look at the pictures and write sentences.**

I'm afraid of ghosts.

I'm not afraid of snakes.

I'm not afraid of cats.

.... spiders.

.... bats.

.... dogs.

✎ **Write and answer the questions.**

Do you like ghosts? Yes, I do.

Do you like snakes? No, I don't.

.... ? ....

.... ? ....

.... ? ....

.... ? ....

Simon de Canterville is a clever[1] ghost. He can change his face and his body! At midnight[2] he makes a horrible face and goes to the twins' bedroom. "OOOHH... AAHHH" says the ghost. But the twins don't wake up[3]!

1. *clever*

2. *midnight*

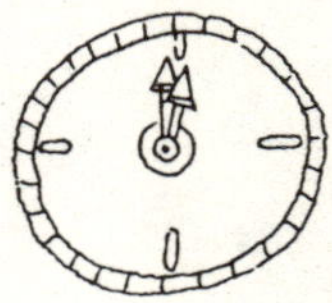

3. *to wake up*

to sleep

ACTIVITY

✎ Write the times.

It's 12 o'clock.

It's ....

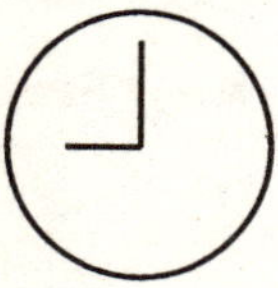

It's ....

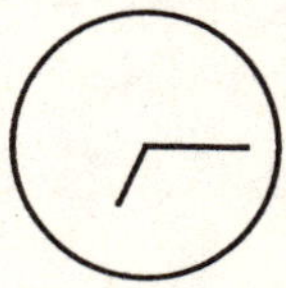

It's ....

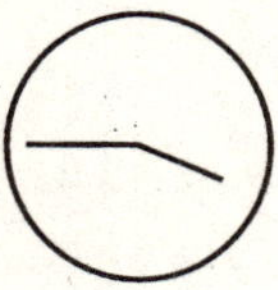

It's ....

It's ....

✎ Write the numbers in the times.

twelve, ...

....

....

"AAHHH!" shouts[1] the ghost again. "I am Simon de Canterville... the terrible ghost!" "We know, we know," yawn[2] the twins. "But we want to sleep now. Go away, Mr Ghost!"

ACTIVITY

✎ **Look at the pictures and write sentences.**

We want to sleep.

sleep

....

eat

....

play

....

study

✎ **Answer the questions about YOU.**

Do you want to sleep? Yes, I do.

Do you want to eat? ....

Do you ....? ....

Do you ....? ....

"I must invent[1] some special effects for these Americans," he thinks. The next night, the ghost puts chains[2] on his wrists[3] and goes to Mr and Mrs Otis's bedroom.

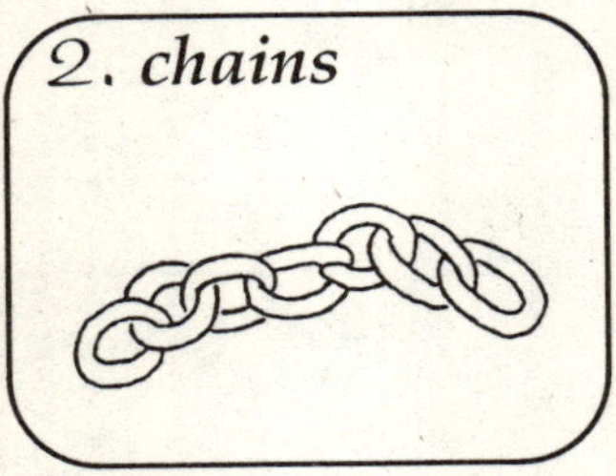

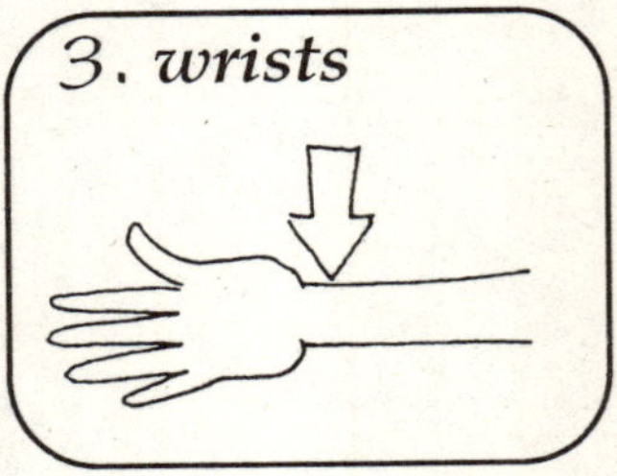

ACTIVITY

✎ TRUE OF FALSE?

	T	F
Simon is a ghost.		
The house is small.		
The Otis family are American.		
Mr Otis puts on chains.		
Simon likes children.		
The ghost is famous.		
The twins are afraid of ghosts.		
The ghost is clever.		

✎ Write the false sentences correctly.

....

....

....

....

"CLANG, CLANG, CLANG!" The chains make a terrible noise! "Wake up!" he shouts. "I am the ghost of the castle!" Mr Otis opens one eye[1]. "Excuse me," says the American. "Please oil[2] your chains. We can't sleep!"

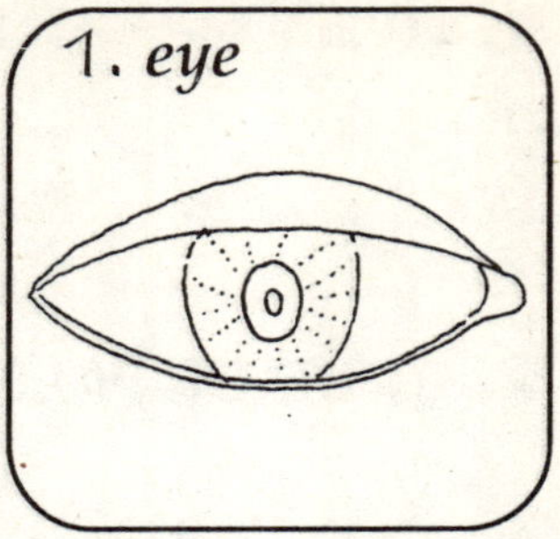

ACTIVITY

✎ **What does the ghost open?**

He opens an eye.

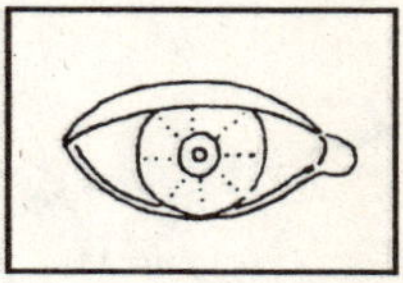

He opens the ....

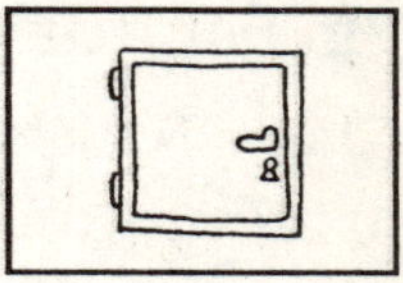

He ....

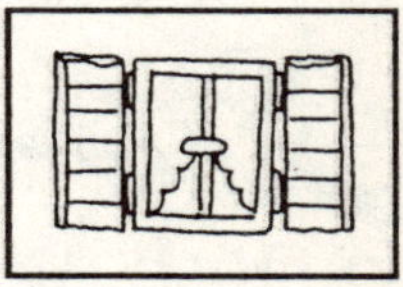

He ....

✎ **Write the sentences in the interrogative.**

Does he open an eye?

....

....

....

Simon de Canterville is furious[1]! On Saturday night he puts on a suit of armour[2] and goes downstairs[3]. "CLONK, CLONK, CLONK!" The Otis family hear the noise and run to the hall.

ACTIVITY

✎ **Write the days of the week.**

Sat	rsday	Saturday
Wed	iday	....
Tue	urday	....
Su	nesday	....
Mon	nday	....
Thu	sday	....
Fr	day	....

✎ **Write the days of the week in the correct order.**

....

....

....

....

"What's this noise?" shout the children at the ghost. "We are children, you know. We have to sleep!"

"AAHHHH," yells[1] Simon de Canterville. The ghost waves[2] his arms to frighten the children but falls[3] down the stairs with a CRASH!

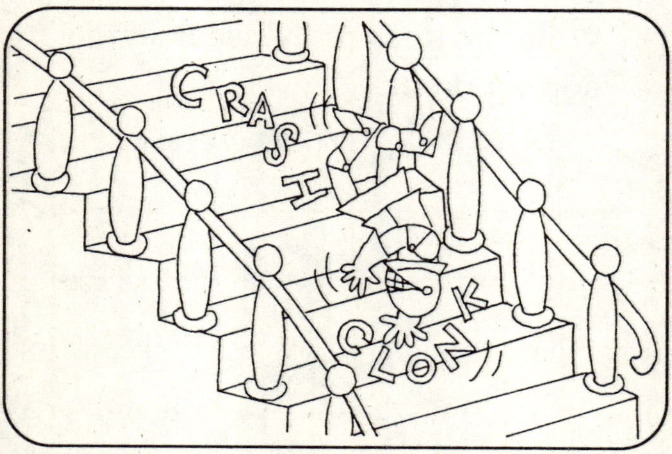

ACTIVITY

✎ **Can you find these words from the story in the grid?**

Sleep, oil, horrible, yawn, clever, noise, children, fall, wave, what, run, body, invent, chain, are, hall, here, must, put, up, goes.

H	Y	C	H	A	I	N	C
O	I	L	L	R	X	O	H
R	M	G	O	E	S	I	I
R	U	S	T	H	V	S	L
I	S	N	A	T	I	E	D
B	T	L	H	N	N	H	R
L	L	J	W	A	V	E	E
E	F	A	L	L	E	R	N
L	Y	D	O	B	N	E	U
S	L	E	E	P	T	U	P

On Sunday, the ghost takes his ghost black cat Fritz to the twins' bedroom. It's a bad[1] cat with big teeth[2] and long claws[3]. "MEIAOO," says Fritz.
"AAHHH," says the ghost.
"HA,HA,HA!" laugh the twins.

1. ***bad*** ***good***

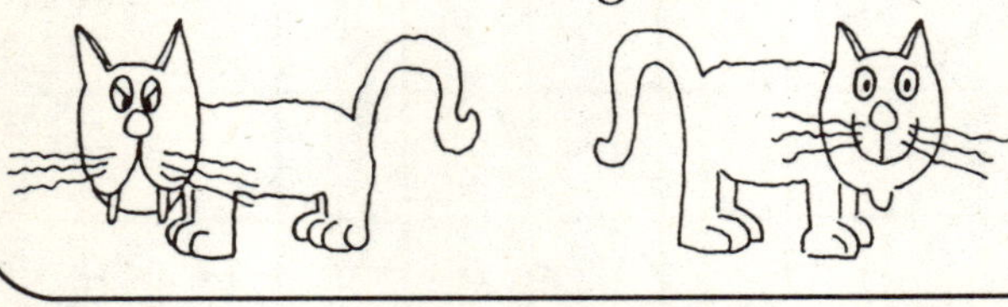

2. ***teeth***

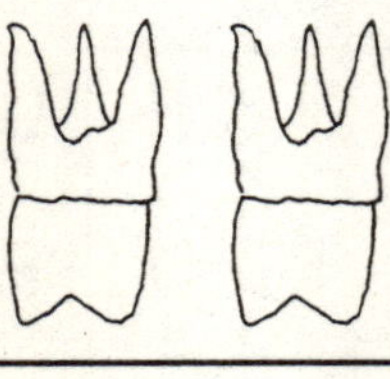

3. ***claws***

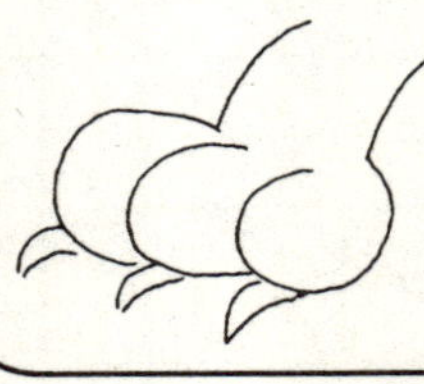

ACTIVITY

✎ **Answer the questions.**

What is the cat's name?

....

What colour is it?

....

Is the cat good?

....

Has it got big teeth?

....

Are its claws long?

....

Are the twins afraid of the cat?

....

Are YOU afraid of cats?

....

The terrible twins throw[1] cold water over Fritz. "MEIAOO," screams the cat and runs away[2]. "My poor cat," thinks Simon de Canterville. "These Americans do not appreciate ghosts."

ACTIVITY

✎ **Complete the following dialogue.**

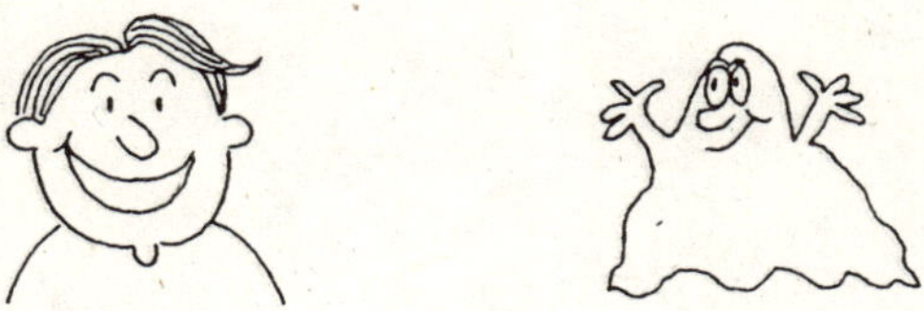

What's your name? My name's Simon.

What are you?

I'm a ....

Where .... live?

In a ....

Have .... cat?

Yes, I ....

What colour ....?

It's ....

What's its ....?

....

Is it a good cat?

No, ... terrible!

On Wednesday the ghost puts on a big red hat[1] and a cloak[2]. He goes to Mary and John's rooms. "AAHHH, AAHHH," he shouts. "Oh dear," says Mary. "Have you got a stomachache[3]? Poor Mr Ghost. Have this medicine[4]. It's very good!"

1. *hat*

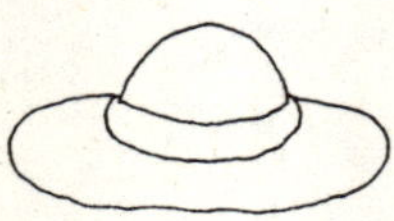

2. *cloak*

3. *stomachache*

4. *medicine*

ACTIVITY

✎ **Fill the gaps and colour the pictures.**

The ghost puts on a green  and a yellow . Then he puts  on his ! "Please 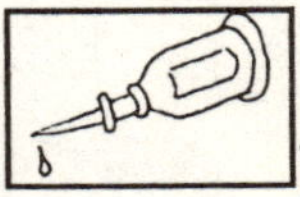 your ," says Mr Otis. "They make a terrible !" "Have you got ?" asks Mrs Otis. "Have this 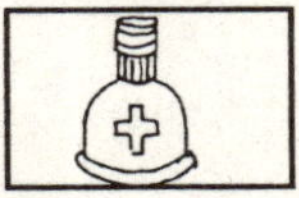. It's very good!" The  waves his 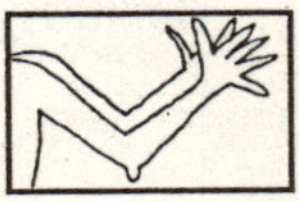 and falls down the 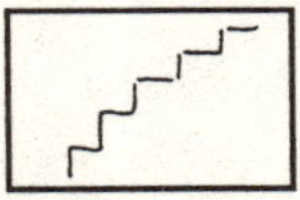!

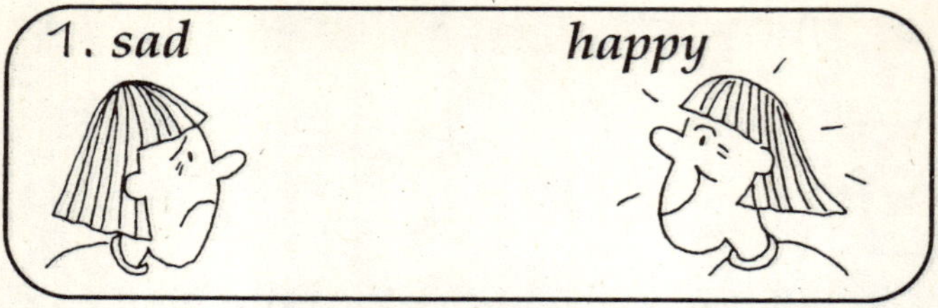

Simon de Canterville is very sad[1]. "These people are not afraid of me. I'm not a good ghost!" Simon sits down and cries[2]. The Otis family are in the sitting room. "Who is crying?" asks Mrs Otis. "Let's go and see," say the twins.

ACTIVITY

✎ **Draw the lines to the house.**

sitting room

bedroom

kitchen

cellar

attic

bathroom

hall

The family go up the stairs to the attic. "Why are you crying?" they ask the ghost. "The ghost inspector arrives[1] tomorrow," cries Simon. "He will see you are not afraid of me. I can't live here if people aren't afraid. It will be terrible!"

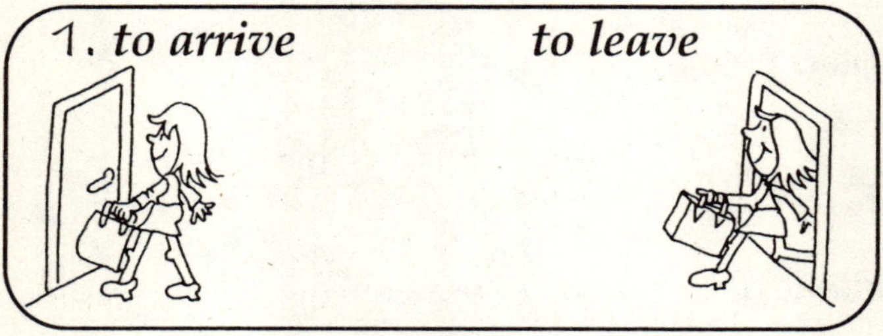

ACTIVITY

Fill the gaps with the double vowels and consonants in the balloon.

oo ll tt tt
oo oo ll

The ghost is in the ce ...... ar.
The twins are in the bathr ...... m.
Mrs Otis is in the kitchen.
Mr Otis is in the si ...... ing r ...... m.
Mary is in the bedr ...... m.
John is in the a ...... ic.
Fritz is in the ha ....

Draw the people in the house on page 25. Colour the picture.

Write four questions.

Where is the ghost ?
Where are ....?
....
....

"We must help him," says Mary. So when the inspector ghost is in the attic, Simon walks down the stairs. "OOOHHH, AAHHH," he shouts. "Help, help," shout the Otis family and run and hide[1]. "Here is the terrible ghost again!" The inspector is very pleased[2] with Simon.

1. *to hide*

2. *pleased*

ACTIVITY

✎ **Write sentences.**

IN

ON

UNDER

The ghost Mary John Mrs Otis The inspector	is isn't	ON IN UNDER	the stairs the chair the table the hall the kitchen

✎ **Write sentences.**

The ghost isn't in the kitchen.

....

....

....

....

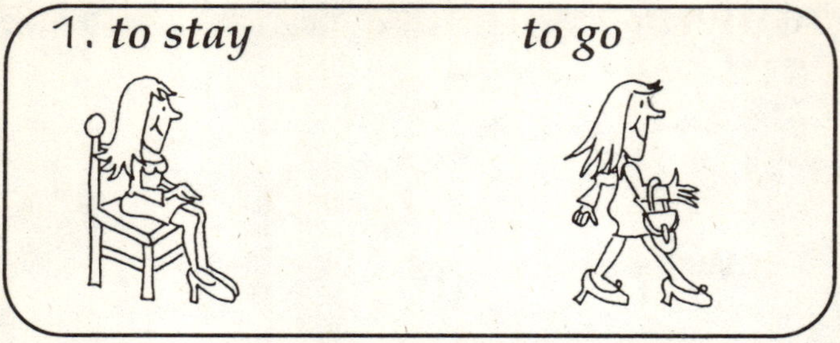

"Excellent!" says the inspector. "This family is really afraid. You can stay[1] in this castle." That night there is a big party at the castle. There is the Otis family and Simon's friends and they live... happily ever after!

ACTIVITY

✎ **Look at the pictures and answer the questions.**

How many cats are there?

There are two cats.

How many ghosts are there?

There is ....

How many ....?

There ....

How many ....?

There ....

How many ....?

There ....